CHRIST'S ETERNAL SONSHIP

by

William Edwy Vine

1873–1949 M.A.

WIPF & STOCK · Eugene, Oregon

Wipf and Stock Publishers
199 W 8th Ave, Suite 3
Eugene, OR 97401

Christ's Eternal Sonship
By Vine, W. E.
Softcover ISBN-13: 978-1-7252-7939-1
Publication date 4/29/2020
Previously published by Pickering & Inglis, 1933

Contents

CHAPTER I

PARALLEL LINES OF DOCTRINE

"The Word" and
"The Only Begotten Son"

CHRIST'S ETERNAL SONSHIP

CHAPTER I

Parallel Lines of Doctrine

PARALLEL lines meet at infinity. That is a fact demonstrable by a geometric proof. It serves as an illustration of the lines of doctrine which set forth the glories of the Son of God. Nowhere does this receive a more striking exposition than in the opening chapter of the Gospel of John. We are at once introduced to this blessed Person as the Eternal Word. The initial declarations concerning Him in this respect lead up to the statement in verse 14, "the Word became flesh and dwelt among us." That leads us along one line of the doctrine.

After an intimation of His Divine relationship, He is brought before us distinctively as the Son of God, and this leads on to His presentation as the Lamb of God. That is the other line of the doctrine, and it runs parallel to the first. Along each our thoughts are taken from Heaven to earth, from eternity into time. Each line takes us to the days of His flesh and to His death. The two lines meet in Him, and so in infinity: for infinite He is, infinite in His Person and in His work. We will consider these two parallels of revelation somewhat more closely.

The Eternal Word.

"In the beginning was the Word, and the Word was with God, and the Word was God" (John 1. 1). The first of these three statements declares His pre-existence. In whatever way the phrase "In the beginning" may be understood (it probably refers to the creation of the Universe), the paramount fact is that He, the Word, was pre-existent to it. Whensoever creation had a beginning He was already there. There was no beginning to His Being.

The second statement declares the distinctiveness of His Person. He was "with God." The preposition is not *sun*, which signifies "accompaniment," nor *meta*, which suggests accompaniment with· mutual interest, but *pros*, which is expressive of a personal attitude towards and occupation with the One Whose presence is being experienced.

The third statement predicates His Deity, His oneness in Godhood with Him Whom the second statement spoke of as God. The three declarations stress the personal nature of Him Who is the Word. That this bears the implication of the existence of two Gods is refuted by this very Gospel, which declares that the Father and the Son are One, and by other Scriptures which predicate that there is one God.*

The Significance of Repetitions.

These initial statements are followed by a repetition of the first and second, with emphasis on the demonstrative pronoun: "The same (or rather, 'This One') was in the beginning with God." But why this repetition? There are no mere repetitions in the Scriptures. Sometimes a reiterated statement is confirmatory of what has been stated; sometimes it is also introductory to what immediately follows.

---

*The same applies to the Holy Spirit. The doctrine of the Unity of the Godhead is prominent in the Old Testament, and is maintained in the New. The New, however, consistently with the progress of doctrine in the Sacred Volume, plainly unfolds the truth of the Tri-unity of Persons in the Unity of the Godhead. A Unitarian recently made the following remark in a conversation with one who holds the truth of the Trinity in Unity: "If what *we* believe is true, you are idolaters; if what *you* believe is true, we are not Christians." Now the doctrine of the Trinity, woven as it is into the very texture of the New Testament, precludes Tritheism and invalidates any imputation of the worship of three Gods. Yet to deny the Deity of Christ is to be devoid of title to be a Christian.

This is the case here; for, immediately after the repeated statement that the Word was in the beginning with God, the existence of the Universe is attributed to Him. "All things were made by Him."

This again is reiterated and expanded: "And without Him was not anything made that hath been made." This also is not simply a repetition. It is preparatory to a declaration that He is the Author of life: life, which exists in Him essentially, is bestowed through Him upon His creatures. "In Him was life, and the life was the light of men." Upon the fact that in Him life is unoriginated and essential rests the dependence of His creatures upon Him for it. The order of life and light is significant. In nature, life in its full activity depends upon light; light is the life of the animate physical creation. In spiritual matters the position is reversed. The Life is the Light. We do not receive spiritual life simply because Christ is the Light. He brings light into our darkness because He brings life, the life that becomes ours when we are born of God, that is to say, when we receive Christ by faith (verse 12).

These subjects, the Word, the Life, and the Light, as set forth in verses 4-13, lead to a resumption of the title "The Word" in verse 14, and to the statement, "The Word became flesh and dwelt among us." The Revisers have rightly rendered by "became" instead of "was made."* The statement that He "became flesh" declares the voluntariness, on the part of Him Who is the Word, of the act of His Incarnation. Further on in the Gospel, as also in the first Epistle of John, we learn that this voluntary act was likewise the sending by the Father. The counsels of grace were mutually designed and carried out; this is true in re-

---

Ginomai should never be rendered "to make," except in the passive voice where English requires it.

spect also of the Holy Spirit, Whose part in the Incarnation is declared in Matthew 1. 18-20 and Luke 1. 35.

The Omission of the Definite Article.

The apostle bears witness for himself and his fellow-apostles that they "beheld His glory, glory as of the only begotten from the Father." There are certain facts to be noted in this phraseology. The definite article is absent in the original before both "only begotten" and "Father." According to a well-known principle in regard to the Greek definite article, its omission before certain descriptions of persons or objects serves to stress the particular feature or character mentioned in the description; whereas, on the other hand, the insertion of the definite article simply points the reader to the person or object as one well known, or one to be recognised. Thus, had the definite articles been used here, the apostle would simply have been pointing out (as is frequently the case) that the two Persons Whom he was mentioning were those well known to his readers as "the only begotten Son" and "the Father." But that is not the case, for he is giving a description of the particular kind of glory which he and his fellow-apostles had seen. The nature of the description, then, shows that the definite articles were purposely omitted in order to lay stress upon the particular characteristics, of the One as an only begotten, and of the Other as a Father.

The Meaning of "Glory."

We may here notice the significance in Scripture of the word "glory," as used of God and of Christ. From what is said in the passages where this word is found, we learn that glory, in this respect, is the manifestation of characteristics or character, and of power. For instance, when in the second chapter we read: "This beginning of His signs" (a sign is a miracle with a meaning or message) did Jesus in Cana of Galilee, and manifested His glory, " the glory which He revealed in His kindly act at the wedding feast was the expression both of His power and His character.

So, then, the glory which the apostles witnessed in Christ was the visible expression of what is indicated in the relationship of "an only begotten from a Father. "

Further, the Revisers have rightly rendered the preposition by "from" and not "of. " The word in the original is "*para*, " which signifies, in this construction, "from the presence of, " "from with (a person). " The same preposition is used in the Lord's own words in 7. 29, "I am from Him, and He sent Me. "

This preposition "from, " together with what has already been set forth concerning the glory as that of a Father's only begotten, indicates that He Who became

flesh, was Himself, in virtue of the previously existing relationship, the unique
and perfect representative and manifestation of the being and character of the
Father from Whose presence He came.
In other words, the glory to which John
refers was the outshining of a unique,
eternal, only begotten sonship. *

The Parallel Line.

Thus far, then, with regard to the first
of the two parallel lines of doctrines in this

---

*That John the Baptist is said to have been "sent from
(*para*) God," does not adversely affect the intimation in
1. 14 that Christ stood prior to His Incarnation in unoriginated relationship as Son to the Father, and that the glory
which the apostles beheld was the glory of One Who held
this relationship.   What requires consideration is both the
contextual phraseology, concerning Christ's glory in its
manifestation in this respect, and the teaching of Scripture
elsewhere concerning the eternal relation between the Father
and the Son.   There is all the difference between the circumstances of the Baptist and what Scripture teaches about
the Person of Christ.   The latter precludes our pressing
the analogy on the ground of the similar use of the preposition.   Angels and prophets are said to stand in the
presence of God, and in this sense John the Baptist was
sent from God, but the truth relating to Christ as "only
begotten from the Father" is different.   *Para* with the
genitive with reference to Him has to do with that which is
antecedent to His birth.

chapter relating to Christ. Now as to the other line, which, as we have mentioned, extends beyond the Prologue into the narrative relating to John the Baptist, while continuing the unfolding of the glory and grace of the Lord Jesus.

In verse 18, He Who was introduced as "the Word" is now spoken of as "the only begotten Son."* For this designation verse 14 has prepared. It was not given as a designation in that verse; for there, as we have observed, the article is omitted.

The Term "Only Begotten."

The term "only begotten," used in verse 18 in connection with the definite article, is one which, with reference to Christ, is found only in the writings of the Apostle John, and, as we have seen in the former

---

*Some manuscripts of considerable authority give the word *theos*, "God," instead of *huios*, "Son," and read "the only-begotten God, the One Being in the bosom of the Father." The Greek words for "God" and "Son" are very similar. The preference, however, is to be given to the word *huios*, "Son."

instance in verse 14, the term does not refer to generation in respect of His Humanity. There are other statements relative to His Sonship which do not contain the title "only begotten," and which do refer to His Incarnation; but that is not the case with *monogenēs*, "only begotten." This speaks of that relationship as Son in which He stands alone, co-equal and eternal with the Father, yet distinct in personality as the Son.

Again, the term as used of the Son's relationship to the Father in the ideal and intimate affections involved therein must be distinguished from generation as applied to human beings. The phrase "eternal generation" finds nothing to correspond to it in Scripture. It does not serve to explain the doctrine of the eternal relationships in the Godhead. Human limitations prevent a full comprehension of the eternal. Yet God has in grace conveyed the facts relating to Himself in language the phraseology of which we can understand, though the facts themselves lie beyond the range of human conception.

The term here, as frequently in Scripture signifies both uniqueness and endearment. Thus of Isaac in Hebrews 11. 17, the writer, quoting from the Septuagint of Genesis 22. 2, instead of from the Hebrew which, translated, reads, "Thy son, thine only son, whom thou lovest, even Isaac, " says that Abraham offered up (lit., "was offering") "his only begotten son. "

Plainly therefore only begotten is in that passage the equivalent of "only. " Now, by actual relationship Isaac was not Abraham's only son. Ishmael had been born before, but Isaac stood in unique relation to Abraham, and in a place of special endearment.

The significance of the word "only begotten, " in a sense altogether apart from birth, is strikingly exemplified in two passages in the Psalms. In that part of Psalm 22 which is anticipatory of the Lord's utterances on the Cross, the appeal is made, "Deliver My soul from the sword, My darling from the power of the dog." According both to the Hebrew and the Greek, the word for "darling" is "only begotten." The same is the case in Psalm 35. 17, where the English translation gives "rescue My soul from their destructions, My darling from the lions." Plainly there can be no connection here with natural relationship of father and son; what is intimated is that that part of the being which is referred to holds the position of preciousness and uniqueness. So with the use of the term in regard to the infinite and unoriginated relationship be-- tween Father and Son.

In addition to the thought of uniqueness and endearment, the term when coupled with the word "Son" conveys the idea of complete representation, the Son manifesting in full expression the characteristics of the Father. This is borne out by what is further said in John 1. 18.

In the Bosom of the Father.

The plain implication of the pre-existent Sonship of Christ given in verse 14 is confirmed in verse 18 by the description of the Son as the One Who is "in the bosom of the Father." The phraseology employed is that of the definite article with the present participle of the verb "to be," lit., "the (One) being in the bosom . . ." This form of phrase provides what is virtually a titular description, and is to be distinguished from the use of the relative pronoun with the present tense of the verb to be ("who is"). Had it been the intention of the writer to state that the Son is at the present time in the bosom of the Father, in contrast to a time in the past when He was not in that position and relationship, the relative clause, that is to say, the relative pronoun with the present tense, would have been used (*i.e.*, *hos esti*, "who is"). The participial construction (the definite article with the present participle "being") is not thus limited in point of time. Here the construction conveys a timeless description, expressing a condition and relationship characteristic, essential and unoriginated.

The phrase "in the bosom of the Father" conveys the thought of affection, and is indicative of the ineffable intimacy and love essentially existent between the Father and the Son, the Son sharing all the Father's counsels, and ever being the object of His love.

The preposition *eis* ("in") expresses something more than the similar preposition *en*. *

---

*Etymologically *eis* (really *ens*) was thus a more comprehensive word than the simple *en*.

What is suggested is not only "in" as indicating the essential union of the Son with the Father, but the further thought of His absolute competency to respond to the Father's love. Of none other could the phrase be used. Nothing is to be gained by rendering the preposition by "into," as if in a more literal sense.

The use of the definite article in this construction points, then, to the uniqueness and the essential nature both of the position and the relationship of Christ.

As in verses 1-14, the doctrines relating to Him as the Word culminate in the statement of His Incarnation, "the Word became flesh," so now verse 18, recalling the description "only begotten" from verse 14, and distinguishing the Son by that designation, leads on, while terminating the Prologue, to the witness of John the Baptist. This is introduced by the particle "and" connecting verse 19 with verse 18, and this witness brings before

us the culminating truth of Christ as
the Lamb of God (verse 29).

The Parallels Reviewed.

There are, on each parallel line of truth
relating to the Person, firstly, a designation
which carries our thoughts back into the
past eternity; and, secondly, a statement
relating to His earthly circumstances.
Thus the lines run, as we have pointed
out, from eternity into time, from Heaven
to earth. At the beginning of the one
line He is made known as "the Word;"
at the beginning of the other as "the only
begotten Son. " These are eternal titles.
Along the first line we are brought to His
Incarnation, with a mention of His grace,
which necessarily includes His death.
Along the second line we are also brought
to the Cross; He Who is "the only begotten
Son" is likewise "the Lamb of God. "
That these two designations are purposively
associated is confirmed from Genesis 22.

where Isaac is spoken of as Abraham's "only son," and where Abraham in the course of his obedience says, "God will provide Himself the Lamb" (verse 8). The typical association is very well known.

On each parallel line, after the essential, unoriginated glories of the Person, as "the Word" and "the only begotten Son," the glories of His grace are revealed. He ("the Word") deigned to become flesh and dwell among us . . . full of grace and truth. He ("the only begotten Son") stooped, as the Lamb of God, to the death of the Cross. Thus "the Word" (verse 1), pre-existent, unoriginated as such, becomes Incarnate (verse 14). The only begotten Son (verse 18), pre-existent, unoriginated as such, is made known as the Lamb of God (verse 29). True, He was foreknown as the Lamb before the foundation of the world (1 Peter 1. 19, 20); but the fact now before us is that He was thus pointed out in the days of His flesh by John the Baptist.

There is another parallel between verses 1 and 18. The significance of the designation "the Word," though an eternal title, finds a correspondence in the statement that the Son "hath declared Him," the Father. The very significance of His title "the Word" lies in His being the means of the communication of Divine thought, the revelation of the mind of God. Similar to this is the fact that, as the Son, He has "declared," has adequately represented Him. As "the Word" He is the revealer of the Divine counsels; as the Son He is the revealer of the Person of the Father.

There is a further parallel. In verse 14 John the Apostle, speaking for himself and his fellow-apostles, says, "We beheld His glory;" in verse 29 John the Baptist, seeing Jesus coming to him, says, "Behold, the Lamb of God, which taketh away the sin of the world;" and again, "Looking upon Jesus as He walked, he says, "Behold, the Lamb of God!" It was initially through John the Baptist's introduction of Christ to the disciples, of whom John, the associate of Peter, was one, that the apostle could afterwards say, "We beheld His glory."

CHAPTER II

———

THE STRESSING OF THE RELATIONSHIPS
(Further Instances)

CHAPTER II

The Stressing of the Relationships

Further Illustrations of the Omitted Article.

THE principle of the stressing of the character or description of a person by means of the omission of the article, as exemplified in the clause "an only begotten from a Father," is well illustrated in certain passages in the Epistle to the Hebrews in connection with the Sonship of Christ.

Hebrews 1. 1, 2.

In the opening words of the Epistle, "God, having of old time spoken unto the fathers in the prophets by divers portions and in divers manners, hath at the end of these days spoken unto us in *His* Son, Whom He appointed Heir of all things, through Whom also He made the worlds, " the insertion of the word "His" in italics is sufficient indication that there is no definite article in the original. Literally, therefore, the statement reads "hath at the end of these days spoken unto us in a Son. " The stress is put upon the relationship. He in Whom God has spoken to us is marked out as One standing in relation to Him as Son to Father. In verse 8, in contrast to this, the article is used: "Of the Son He saith, Thy throne, O God, is for ever and ever. " The use of the definite article here marks the Son as the Person Who has already been spoken of in this respect.

The design in the stress on the word "Son" in verse 2 is not to convey the idea that God has spoken to us in One Who became His Son, but that He has done so in One Whose relationship to

Him as Son stands in antecedent existence both to creation and to His Incarnation. The appointment of Christ as Heir was a matter of the Divine counsels in Eternity.

The passage is itself a testimony to the pre-existent Sonship of Christ; for not only has God spoken to us in Him Who is His Son, but by Him, "the Heir of all things," He "made the worlds" (the ages). The plain implication is that He by Whom God made the worlds stood in relationship to Him in this respect as His Son. If there was no such relationship before the Incarnation, the conclusion seems unavoidable that one God made use of another God to make the worlds. There are not two Gods, nor are there three acting together. Deity is monotheistic. He by Whom all things were created (Col. 1. 16), was the Son of the Father's love (verse 13), and one with Him in Godhood as Creator as in all other attributes of Deity. See further in chapter 5.

The Father, the Son, and the Holy
Spirit were never three separate Beings
each possessed of the attributes of Deity,
each self-existent, and possessed of similar
character and power. That there is only
one God remains an essential doctrine of
the Christian Faith. That there are three
distinct Persons in the Godhead is con-
sistent with the foundation truth of the
unity of the Godhead. The very titles
given in Scripture are evidences of this.
Yet each is God, that is to say, possessed
of Godhood, and all subsist together as
the One God. Denial of the eternal Sonship of Christ lays one open to the Tri-
theistic idea that, as to presence, place,
and glory, Divine Persons were together,
co-equal and co-eternal, and yet that
the Father and the Son were not related
as Father and Son. It leads also to the
erroneous view that the relationships of
the Father and the Son belong simply to
the sphere of revelation (see page 59).

It will be helpful here to quote Liddon's remarks on the use of the word *Persons* in reference to the Father, the Son, and the Holy Spirit. Speaking of the truth relating to the Godhead, he says: "It postulates the existence in God of certain real distinctions having their necessary basis in the essence of the Godhead. That such distinctions exist is a matter of Revelation. . . . These distinct forms of being are named Persons. Yet that term cannot be employed to denote Them, without considerable intellectual caution. As applied to men, persons implies the antecedent conception of a species, which is determined for the moment, and by the force of the expression, into a single, incommunicable modification of being. But the conception of species is utterly inapplicable to That One Supreme Essence which we name God; the same Essence belongs to each of the Divine Persons. Not, however, that we are therefore to suppose nothing more to be intended by the revealed doctrine than three varying relations of God in His dealings with the world. On the contrary, His self-revelation has for its basis certain eternal distinctions in His nature, which are themselves altogether anterior to and independent of any relation to created life. Apart from these distinctions, the Christian Revelation of an Eternal Fatherhood, of a true incarnation of God, and of a real communication of His Spirit, is but the baseless fabric of a dream. These three distinct 'Subsistences,' which we name Father, Son, and Spirit, while they enable us the better to understand the mystery of the Self-sufficing and Blessed Life of God before He surrounded Himself with created beings, are also strictly compatible with the truth of the Divine Unity. And when we say that Jesus Christ is God, we mean that in the Man Christ Jesus the second of these Persons or Subsistences, one in essence with the First and with the Third, vouchsafed to become Incarnate. "

The Omitted Definite Article in Hebrews 1. 5.

Again, in Hebrews 1. 5, in the quotation, "I will be to Him a Father, and He shall be to Me a Son," the omission of the definite article places the emphasis upon the relationship expressed in the terms "Father" and "Son." This statement is not a prediction about a time when the relationship would begin. The beginning of the relationship is not in view. What is set forth is, firstly, its distinct character in contrast to its non-existence in the case of the angels; and secondly, the adequate realisation of it in His life of entire obedience to the Father's will; and not only then, but its continuance ever afterwards. The relationship which had eternally existed found a new expression in the Son Incarnate.

There is a love which had no beginning, involved in the relationship. Never
would the love of the Father to the Son
and that of the Son to the Father have
become known and adoringly apprehended
by the redeemed, had it not been for the
Incarnation of the Son. The manifestation of the relationship gives us to appre-
ciate in measure what the Father is to the
Son and what the Son is to the Father.
In the statement, then, "I will be to Him
a Father, and He shall be to Me a Son,"
we have the assurance that the relationship
was to be realised in a perpetual fulfilment
in the Divine actings on behalf of man,
and in an ineffable appreciation therein
of the Fatherhood of the Father by the
Son, and of the Sonship of the Son by the
Father.

The word *huios*, "son," is not simply,
nor indeed always, indicative of offspring;
it signifies expression of character. We
read, for instance, of "sons of this world,"

and "sons of light" (Luke 16. 8, R.V.). Used of the Lord Jesus, the single title "Son" generally signifies, as in the passages we have just considered regarding Him, that He shares in unoriginated subsistence the Father's nature, and is the revealer of His character. Thus He says to Philip, "He that hath seen Me hath seen the Father" (John 14. 9). Plainly what is in view in such a statement is not the inception of the relationship.

For further illustrations of the omission of the definite article in this respect, in the Epistle to the Hebrews, see 5. 8 and 7. 28.

CHAPTER III

———

HIS SONSHIP AS
THE SENT ONE

CHAPTER III

His Sonship as the Sent One

THERE are many passages which speak of the Sonship of Christ in respect of His having been the One sent by the Father; these call for our contemplation, especially in connection with what is involved as to the glory and grace of our blessed Lord. The first of these in the Gospel of John is in chapter 3, verses 16 and 17: "For God so loved the world, that He gave His only begotten Son, that whosoever believeth on Him should not perish, but have eternal life. For God sent not the Son into the world to judge the world, but that the world should be saved through Him." Neither does this Scripture nor any other state that it was as the Son of God in Manhood that He was given and sent (see on Gal. 4. 4, p. 54). The statement does not mean that the sending into the world took place after His birth and His having grown up into Manhood. Both the gift and the sending were from Heaven. The greatness of the love of God in giving and sending is measured in terms of the pre-existent relationship expressed in the title "only begotten."

That the Lord was in the presence of Nicodemus when He spoke of Himself in this way provides no support for the view that the sending into the world was subsequent to His birth. Nor again does the fact that John the Baptist began his public career as a man sent from God afford an analogy for the sending of Christ in the same way. John had no antecedent existence; Christ was eternally pre-existent.

Nor does the fact that Christ came in a Mediatorial character provide an argument against His pre-existent Sonship. His relation as Son to the Father is not con-

tingent upon His Mediatorship. On the
contrary, as we shall see from Colossians
1. 15, 18, His Mediatorial acts, in regard
both to creation and redemption, were
consequent upon His already existing
Sonship.

"Sanctified and Sent."

In His controversy with the Jews the
Lord speaks of Himself as the One "Whom
the Father sanctified and sent into the
world" (John 10. 6). The order is significant, and is sufficient to show, when
taken with other Scriptures, that the
sending was from Heaven to earth. The
order is "sanctified and sent," not "sent
and sanctified." The sanctification, that
is, the setting apart for the purpose, was
not a matter of time. It was in the
counsels of God before the foundation of
the world, that the Son was set apart for
His mission of redeeming grace.

The testimony in 1 John 4. 9, 10 concerning God's love to us can only rightly

be understood in the same way: "Herein was the love of God manifested in us, that God hath sent His only begotten Son into the world, that we might live through Him. Herein is love, not that we loved God, but that He loved us, and sent His Son to be the propitiation for our sins." The love of the Father for the Son, implied in the term "only begotten," was a love of which the Son Himself, in addressing the Father as the Father, says: "Thou lovedst Me before the foundation of the world" (John 17. 24). If that pre-existent love was not between the Father and the Son, what can have been the relationship in which it was exercised? It does not suffice that the Divine Persons were co-equal and co-eternal. God did not send One Who was simply God.

Pre-existent Glory with the Father.

The love involved in the relationship

prior to the Incarnation marks the sending as taking place, not out into public life after Christ had grown up, but from the glory of which He says, "And now, O Father, glorify Thou Me with Thine own self with the glory which I had with Thee before the world was" (17. 5). Such words are surely a testimony against an interpretation that the glory which was His was with One Who eventually became His Father when He was born. True, we cannot define that glory, but we can accept the truth of the eternal existence of the relationship and the eternal love involved in it. That He received honour and glory from the Father in the days of His flesh affords no testimony to the contrary. So again the apostle's statement, "We have beheld and bear witness that the Father hath sent the Son to be the Saviour of the world" (1 John 4. 14), does not mean that having become the Father, He sent the One Who had become His Son to be the Saviour of the world (see on Galatians 4. 4, below).

His Sonship Essential in His Godhood.

It is evident from the Lord's prayer recorded in John 17 that His relationship as the Son to the Father subsists essentially in His Divine personality. His Sonship, therefore, must have subsisted in the Eternal Godhead, and unchangeably so, for a change in His Godhood is impossible.

The pre-existent relationship is expressed in the Lord's words in John 16. 28: "I came out from the Father, and am come into the world: again, I leave the world and go unto the Father." The twofold course, both in the coming and the return, is clear. His return to the Father was in the reverse order of procedure to that of His coming. He came from Heaven to the world; He returned from the world to

Heaven. He speaks of the One from Whom He came as "the Father," not in the sense that He came out from One Who subsequently became the Father at His birth, but from One Who was the Father when He came out. Nor can His statements mean that His coming into the world was an entrance into public life, as in His Manhood, after God has become His Father. His leaving the world, by way of His exaltation to the Father's right hand, was in direct antithesis to the stoop which He took when, coming forth from the glory which He had with the Father, He humbled Himself to become Incarnate.

An Analogy Concerning the Holy Spirit.
(Galatians 4. 4-6).

The word "sent forth" is used both of the Son and of the Holy Spirit in Galatians 4. 4-6: "When the fulness of the time came,

God sent forth His Son, born of a woman,
born under the Law, that He might
redeem them which were under the Law,
that we might receive the adoption of sons.
And because ye are sons, God sent forth
the Spirit of His Son into our hearts,
crying, Abba, Father."

The use of the word "send" with reference to the Holy Spirit throws light upon
the significance of the word as used of the
sending of the Son by the Father. The
Lord said that the Father would send the
Holy Spirit, and that He Himself would
likewise do so. He was not the Holy
Spirit because He was sent; He did not
become the Holy Spirit upon the occasion
of His mission. So neither did Christ
become the Son in being sent from the
Father.

The analogy, then, confirms the pre-
existent Sonship of Christ. But not only
so, the very title, "the Spirit of His Son,"
expresses that essential relation and

characteristic of the Holy Spirit with regard to the Son by reason of which He produces the spirit of sonship within us.

Even grammatically, the statement may not be read as if it meant that "God sent forth His Son, having been born of a woman. " The construction in the original is against such a rendering. The construction is precisely the same, for instance, as in Philippians 2. 8, where "becoming" translates the same word as that here rendered "born" (*ginomai*), the form of the verb being the same. The statement, "He humbled Himself, becoming obedient even unto death, " could not mean that He humbled Himself after having become obedient unto death. On the contrary, His self-humbling was expressed in His becoming obedient. The particular form of the verb rendered "becoming" signifies the mode of the humbling.

So the preceding verse, where the same

word is rendered "being made," sets forth the mode of His self-emptying. "He emptied Himself, taking the form of a servant, becoming in (see *margin*) the likeness of men." He did not empty Himself after taking the form of a servant and becoming in the likeness of men. These acts specify how His self-emptying* took effect.

This construction, then, throws light upon the statement in Galatians 4. 4. The clause, "born of a woman," particularises the act, not the antecedent, of the sending. He was not sent forth after His birth. The sending forth took effect in His birth. The One Who was sent forth was already the Son of the Father. He was and is the Son, not because He began to derive this relation-

---

*The construction is the aorist participle following a main predicate in the past tense. The aorist (or indefinite) participle in such a construction does not mark an event which took place prior to that expressed by the preceding verb; it serves to specify the mode of the action signified by that predicate.

ship from the Father at His Incarnation, but because He ever was, in that relationship, the expression of what the Father is, as confirmed in His own statement, "He that hath seen Me hath seen the Father" (John 14. 9).

Relationship not Determined by Revelation.

The fact that no names such as "the Son," "the Son of God," were actually given till the New Testament in no way serves to disprove the pre-existent relationship. Did not Jehovah, for instance, exist as Jehovah before the title was revealed to man? Was God, "the Almighty God," simply from the time when He first made Himself known by this title? Does His existence as the Father begin simply from the time when that title was revealed to man? Far from it. The existence of the attributes and character of God, and the relation of the Son to the

Father, did not depend upon their revelation to man.   Certainly it is because God has made Himself known as the Father, and has provided the means by which we become His children, that we can regard Him in that relationship and through grace can address Him so.   But that fact does not afford us any ground for the supposition that He was not the Father till He was made known in that relationship.   Neither are we to suppose that Christ was the Son only when He was revealed as Son, any more than God was God only when He was made known as such.   Facts of Deity are not contingent upon human knowledge. To regard the relationship of Fatherhood and Sonship as being contingent upon the revelation of the Persons in the Godhead to creatures, is to conceive of the subject in the reverse order of that revealed in Scripture.   The eternal relationship of the Father to the Son was entirely compatible with the equality of the Persons

in the Godhead.   It was compatible, too,
with the fact that God as God is invisible,
and with the truth of the inscrutability
of the Godhead as such.

Subordination not Inferiority.

The question arises whether the position
of subjection which Christ took in His life
of perfect obedience to the Father involved
His inferiority in the Divine relationship.
Now, even in earthly relationships sonship
does not necessarily involve inferiority.
When a son is grown up to manhood, and
undertakes responsibilities which formerly
belonged to his father, he is frequently in
a position of equality with his father.
Solomon was king of Israel while yet his
father David was alive.   If this may be so
in human relationships, how must more
in regard to relationships in the Godhead?
Christ became subordinate in His Incarnation for the purpose of the fulfilment of
the Father's will, and in Divine grace

towards man, but His subordination did not involve His inferiority, as the Son of God. In becoming Man He did not abrogate His attributes of Deity. In His birth, and without intermission, His Godhood remained. Accordingly He said, "I and the Father are one" (John 10. 30), and enjoined that all were to honour the Son "even as they honour the Father, " declaring likewise that "he that honoureth not the Son honoureth not the Father which sent Him" (5. 23).

If in human affairs the sending of a person may mean authority on the part of the sender and inferiority on the part of him who is sent, we are not justified in pressing the analogy to hold good in the case of Divine Persons. For the fact remains that in absolute Deity the Son, as such, was sent by the Father, as such, into the world, without any change in equality of the Persons as in the Godhead. The fact of the eternal equality does not render the relationship, and what was involved in the sending, incompatible with the continued equality, in respect of Deity.

The same is true of the Holy Spirit. In Deity He always was and ever remained on equality with the Father and with the Son, and yet the Holy Spirit was sent at Pentecost both by the Father and by the Son (John 14. 26; 15, 26; 16. 7). The sending did not involve inferiority in His case. In regard, therefore, to the Persons in the Godhead, the term "sent" does not imply such a relative position as is inconsistent with equality in Deity.

The new condition into which Christ entered in becoming Man was, indeed, one of subordination (Heb. 2. 9; 5. 8; cp. 1 Cor. 15. 27). Accordingly He said, "My Father is greater than I" (John 14. 28). With this statement we may compare His word concerning His sheep: "My Father, which hath given them unto

Me, is greater than all" (John 10. 29).
The context in each passage shows that
there is a difference. The statement in
10. 29 is not relative to the Son as Incarnate, but is absolute. For He says
that the sheep are as secure in His hand
as they are in the Father's (verse 28), and
proceeds to say, "I and the Father are
one" (verse 30). In 14. 28, however,
the context points to the statement, "My
Father is greater than I," as being relative
to the Son as Incarnate. Here the Lord
has in view His return to the Father.
He would then enter into a glory which
He had not in the days of His flesh. He
is regarding His return in the light of the
completion of what He came to do in His
servant character, and in fulfilment of the
Father's will. His subordination in the
days of His flesh did not therefore involve
His inferiority.

Chapter IV

"THOU ART MY SON, THIS DAY HAVE I BEGOTTEN THEE"

CHAPTER IV

"Thou art My Son, this Day have I Begotten Thee"

Psalm 2. 7 and its Quotations.
The First Quotation:
Acts 13. 33.

THE declaration, "Thou art My Son, this day have I begotten Thee," quoted in Acts 13. 33; Hebrews 1. 5, and 5. 5, from Psalm 2. 7, indicates a distinct act accomplished at a given time. As to the occasion referred to, the context both in Acts 13 and Hebrews 1 gives intimations. In Acts 13 Paul is addressing the men of Israel in the synagogue at Antioch in Pisidia; in briefly narrating the history of the people, he speaks of David as having been "raised up" to be their king (verse 22). Obviously not resurrection

from the dead is there in view, but the raising up of a person through birth and
childhood into manhood, to occupy a
particular position in the nation.   In the
same sense Moses had spoken of Christ as
follows: "The Lord thy God will raise up
unto thee a Prophet from the midst of
thee, of thy brethren, like unto me."
This is quoted by the apostle Peter in
addressing the people in Solomon's Porch
(Acts 3. 22), and by Stephen in addressing
the Council (7. 37).   This prophecy received its fulfilment in that Christ was
raised up as a Prophet in the nation as the
result of His Incarnation.   That ministry
He fulfilled in the days of His flesh.

In Acts 13. 33, the apostle Paul speaks
in the same way in the synagogue at
Antioch concerning Christ.   He says:
"We bring you glad tidings of the promise
made unto the fathers, how that God hath
fulfilled the same unto our children, in
that He raised up Jesus" (verse 33).

That is to say, God raised Him up in the midst of the nation in the same sense as in the other passages just noted. The word "again" in the A.V. has nothing corresponding to it in the original. The translators of the A.V. added the word "again" by way of interpretation. The reference in this verse (unlike that in the next), is not to resurrection, but to what has already been stated. In verse 34 the additional statement of His resurrection is made with stress upon it: "And as concerning that He raised Him up from the dead, now no more to return to corruption, He hath spoken on this wise, I will give you the holy and sure blessings of David." His having been raised from the dead stands thus in emphatic contrast to, and as the counterpart of, what was stated in verse 33 as to His being raised up in the nation. Emphasis is imparted by the addition of the words "from the dead."

Now in verse 33 the statement as to the raising up of Jesus in the midst of the nation is confirmed by the quotation from the second Psalm: "Thou art My Son, this day have I begotten Thee." Accordingly, the reference in this quotation would be to His Incarnation. The order is significant: His Incarnation in verse 33, His resurrection from the dead in verse 34. In these two respects the apostle says that God both has fulfilled His promise made unto the fathers, and has given the sure blessings of David.

The Second Quotation:
Hebrews 1. 5.

That the reference in the declaration, "Thou art My Son, this day have I begotten Thee," is to the Incarnation, is confirmed by the quotation in Hebrews 1. 5, and its relation to the 6th verse. The clause, "And when He again bringeth in the Firstborn into the world" (R.V.) looks on to the Second Advent (see Chapter V, in connection with the subject of Christ as the Firstborn). That event, yet future, is set in contrast to the birth of Christ, His First Advent. It was then that God brought His Firstborn into the world the first time. To this, accordingly, the quotation refers in the preceding verse, "Thou art My Son, this day have I begotten Thee."

What is stated in regard to the Incarnation in this declaration can only rightly be viewed in the light of the existent and eternal relationship of the Father to the Son. This pre-existent relationship found expression in that act of grace by which the Son became Man through the operation of the Holy Spirit according to the counsels of the Triune God.

That the Lord Jesus was the Son of God in that special phase of His existence by which He "partook of flesh and blood" (Heb. 2, 14), being born of the Virgin Mary,

does not involve His not having pre-
existed in relationship as Son to the
Father. That act, accomplished with
the purposes of redemption in view, was
effected by those who stood the One to the
Other in unoriginated relationship and
Divine nature as Father and Son, as well
as by the Holy Spirit. The declaration,
"Thou art My Son, this day have I begotten Thee," was made in view of the fact
that now, in the scheme of redemption,
He Who was the Son had become Incarnate, combining in Himself humanity
and Deity.

His Incarnation constituted a new and
distinct phase in the existence of Him Who,
in unoriginated personality in the Godhead, was antecedently "the only begotten
Son in the bosom of the Father." That
pre-existent relationship but enhances
the glory of the grace of His Incarnation.
His had been the eternal glory which He
had with the Father, and His was now

the additional glory of that condescending grace by which He stooped to become Man. The very infinitude of His Person in relationship to the Father forbids the deduction that, because the Father, in view of what took place at Bethlehem, said, "Thou art My Son, this day have I begotten Thee," His Sonship therefore began at that time.

The Third Quotation: Hebrews 5. 5.

The third quotation is set in connection with the High Priesthood of Christ, which forms the central theme of the Epistle. It was introduced at the beginning of the third chapter, and is continued from the 14th verse of the fourth chapter into the fifth, and from the seventh to the tenth. In chapters 5 and 7 two points stand out prominently in the presentation of the perfect fitness of the Lord Jesus for His High Priestly ministry.

The one relates to His Incarnation, His experiences in the days of His flesh, His death and resurrection and exaltation. The other relates to the eternal character of His Sonship.

In regard to the first, and with a view to expanding the character of the Priesthood of Christ, the writer shows how He fulfilled all that was foreshadowed concerning Him in the Levitical priesthood (chapter 5. 1-4). Two qualifications marked the high priest of old. He was taken from among men, and was appointed by God for man (verse 1). This was fulfilled in the Person of the Lord Jesus Christ. He became Man, and has been appointed by God the Father: "and no man taketh the honour unto himself, but when he is called of God, even as was Aaron. So Christ also glorified not Himself to be made a High Priest, but He that spake unto Him, Thou art My Son, this day have I begotten Thee" (vv. 4, 5).

The passage stresses the fact of His humanity, the days of His flesh, His strong crying and tears, His perfect obedience as Son, and His sufferings. His sacrificial death was the foundation upon which He perfectly fulfils His office as High Priest.

The Melchizedek Character of His Priesthood.

But this further is added, that His priesthood is not after the Aaronic order, but after the order of Melchizedek (vv. 6-10). This subject is extended at the close of the 6th chapter and the beginning of the 7th.

Now it is in connection with the Melchizedek character of the Lord's High Priesthood that His eternal Sonship is intimated. For Melchizedek is "made like unto the Son of God" in this, that he stands before us in the Genesis record, "without father, without mother, without genealogy, having neither beginning of days nor end of life" (Heb. 7. 3). If the Sonship of the Lord began at His Incarnation, then the analogy fails in the respect that He had beginning of days at His birth. It is significant that in this comparison He is called "the Son of God," for only just before, in 6. 20, He is spoken of simply as "Jesus," and at the beginning of the chapter as "Christ." The title "Son of God" is purposely chosen in order that, this relationship being presented, He may, in not having beginning of days or end of life, fulfil the analogy with Melchizedek. The very glory of Christ's High Priesthood lies in this, that He stands in His relationship as the Son of God, and that in this respect He has neither beginning of days nor end of life. It was an obligation with the Aaronic priests to declare their genealogy, but Melchizedek stands before us in the narrative in Genesis not only with an absence of these details, but likewise without mention of human parentage, and in this his likeness to the Son of God also exists.

It is in His Divine relationship, then, to the Father, that Christ has neither beginning of days nor end of life. This stands in striking contrast to the period spoken of as "the days of His flesh" (5. 7), which began with His birth and ended with His death. But that is not the case with His Sonship, and in this respect it is a significant feature of the Gospel of John, the object of which is to present Him as the Son of God, that it gives no record of His birth.

Thus the perfections of our High Priest lie in this, among other respects, that He is possessed both of Godhood and Manhood. His Deity is set forth in the Hebrews Epistle, as well as in other Scriptures, in that He was the Son of God, not simply in time but in the eternal past; His humanity is set forth in this that, being already the Son of the Father, He became Man by an act of grace, being "born of a woman" by Divine operation. This stupendous condescension received the Divine declaration, "Thou art My Son, this day have I begotten Thee."

It is true that the word "eternal" is not used in Scripture in connection with the Sonship of Christ, but that affords no proof that the relationship did not exist in the eternal past. Phraseology that is endorsed by the general teaching of Scripture is sound, and the Scriptures give abundant evidence that the relationship was eternal.

CHAPTER V

THE SIGNIFICANCE OF THE TITLE
"THE FIRSTBORN"

CHAPTER V

The Significance of the Title " The Firstborn "

(i) The Firstborn with Reference to Creation.

THERE is a significant passage which, like the 1st chapter of the Gospel of John, speaks both of His Creatorship and of His relationship with the Father, and teaches plainly that He gave Creation its being in virtue of His pre-existent Sonship. This is Colossians 1. 16, 17, where Christ is described as "the image of the invisible God, the Firstborn of all Creation."*

It is necessary first to consider the objective character of the phrase "of all creation." We say "objective" in contrast to "subjective," as if He were

---

*For a paper on the subject see "Echoes of Service," October, 1910; also a booklet, "Christ the Firstborn."

Himself the subject of creative power, and so were to be classed with Creation; whereas, on the contrary, the construction is plainly objective, signifying that the Universe owes its existence to Him as its Creator. This is confirmed by the succeeding context, which declares that "all things were created by Him, things visible and invisible, whether thrones or dominions or principalities or powers." Accordingly, to class Him with Creation is to imply that He created Himself, which is an absurdity. The phrase means, then, that as the Firstborn He was the Producer of Creation. *

---

*This objective genitive construction is quite frequent in the N.T. Thus in John 2. 17, "the zeal of Thine House" means "the zeal for Thine House." In John 10. 7, "the door of the sheep" signifies "the door for the sheep to enter by." Acts 4. 9 literally reads, "the good deed of an impotent man," which plainly is "the good deed done to an impotent man." In John 17. 2, where, literally, the phrase is "authority of all flesh," the only possible rendering is "authority over all flesh." There is a further striking example of the objective genitive in the description of Christ as "the Beginning of the creation of God" (Rev. 3. 14, see page 90). This does not class Him with the creation referred to there, but speaks of Him as the Originator, the prime Cause and Head of it.

We may note, in passing, the three prepositions in verse 16. The R.V. gives these correctly: "All these things have been created in Him . . . through Him, and unto Him." The first preposition "in" signifies that He personally was the centre of the Divine counsels concerning Creation before it actually had being, just as an architectural design exists in the mind of the architect before the actual building is constructed. The second preposition "through" marks Him as Himself the instrument in bringing Creation into existence. The third, "unto," signifies that He is the object for Whose glory the Universe has been brought into being.

The Term "Firstborn."

The term "firstborn," while sometimes used in Scripture in its literal sense, is, on the contrary, frequently used without reference to primogeniture, and in order to indicate pre-eminence. This is clear, for instance, from the Mosaic Law in Deuteronomy 21. 16, which decreed that a man who had two wives, the one beloved and the other hated, who had both borne him children, must not, when dividing his inheritance among his sons, "make the son of the beloved the firstborn before the son of the hated, which is the firstborn. " Clearly the term is used to signify a position of pre-eminence or headship above others. Sometimes indeed the word is used without reference to natural birth at all. Thus God says to Pharaoh, "Israel is My son, My firstborn" (Exod. 4. 22). Again, in Jeremiah 31. 9, He speaks in the same way of Ephraim : "I am a Father to Israel, and Ephraim is My firstborn. "

Now, while the term does involve the relationships of fatherhood and sonship, yet the passages in Exodus and Jeremiah are sufficient to illustrate the fact that with reference to the Lord Jesus Christ the title does not refer to any inception of His relationship to the Father. On the contrary, it is used to signify His priority and His pre-eminence over created beings. It marks Him as the ideal pattern to which they were designed to conform.

The Firstborn of all Creation.

The form of expression illustrated by the phrase "Firstborn of all Creation" was frequently used to distinguish a person from others in declaring his priority to them in time, and his superiority over them in position. The literal rendering, for instance, of the words of John the Baptist in John 1. 15, 30, is: "He was the first of Me." Now John expressly combats the idea that he himself was the Christ, and certainly the phrase he used does not class Christ with the order of beings to which He Himself belonged. So the Greek historian Xenophon speaks of a war as "the most notable of wars previously waged." The "of" clearly implies distinction, not association. For a war is not itself of a number of those waged before it. In English literature, too, this distinctive use of the word "of" may be illustrated by Milton's line, "Adam, the goodliest man of men since born." Adam was not one of the men born after him, so the "of" is again used in the sense of distinction, not identification.

Just so Christ, as the Firstborn, is distinct from and prior to all created beings, and the phrase marks His superiority over them as their Creator. In the phrase, "the Firstborn of all Creation," however, the special import is not only His priority to and pre-eminence over Creation, but His relationship to the Father while acting as Creator.

Merely temporal priority is to be excluded from the phrase in this verse. Headship is the dominant idea, but this again not without that of the essential, and therefore unoriginated relationship to the Father. The phrase, and indeed the passage itself, show that in the creation of the Universe Christ acted not only in virtue of His Godhead, but as the Son accomplishing His work for the glory of the Father. The term "Firstborn" beautifully combines, as no other term would do, the two subjects, both that of His relationship to the Father and that of His Headship over Creation. His resurrection is not here in view, for it was not in resurrection that He became the Firstborn. Nor did the natural Creation owe its existence to Him in virtue of His prospective resurrection from the dead.

The Five Passages Viewed Chronologically.

With the term "Firstborn" as thus used in Colossians 1. 15, we may connect the four other places where it is used of Christ. We will take them according to the chronological order of the events connected with the title. The first has to do, as we have noticed, with His work as Creator. The second and third have reference to His death and resurrection. The fourth is associated with His position among His saints in their future glorified state; the fifth with the manifestation of His Person and glory at His Second Advent.

(ii) The Term "Firstborn" in Connection with His Resurrection
(*First Aspect*).
Colossians 1. 18.

In verse 18 of this first chapter of Colossians, Christ is called "The Firstborn from the dead." While verse 15 speaks of His power and Headship in regard to the natural Creation, this verse speaks of the same in regard to the spiritual: "He is the Head of the Body, the Church: Who is the Beginning, the Firstborn from the dead; that in all things He might have the pre-eminence."

This does not imply that Christ entered upon this relationship to the Father either at His birth or in His resurrection. Just as in regard to the Creation, so His was priority in resurrection. Unlike others previously raised, He has been raised to die no more.

That He is the Firstborn from the dead does not imply that He was the Firstborn because He has been raised from the dead. What is conveyed in the phrase is the fact that, had He not been raised from the dead, no others could have had resurrection, and the Church could never have been brought into being. Again, as we have seen with regard to the natural Creation, the term combines the twofold idea of His unoriginated relationship to the Father and His Headship over the spiritual Creation.

"The Beginning."

Further, in connection with His saints,

as the Firstborn from the dead He is here called "The Beginning." In His resurrection lie the source and potentiality of their spiritual life; His resurrection is the pledge and earnest of theirs. That He is the Firstborn with regard to them is not a matter of primogeniture, but of superiority to and Headship over them, the object being that "in all things He might have the pre-eminence." In relation to the Church, He is the Source and Creator of the spiritual life of the saints who form His Body. As the Head He rules, guides, unites, sustains them; He is the mainspring of their energy and the power of their activity.

With reference to the new Creation, the Lord speaks of Himself as "the Beginning of the Creation of God," in addressing the Laodicean church (Rev. 3. 14). As already observed in connection with the objective sense of the phrase, He is not Himself included in that which is created, but being Divinely appointed in the counsels of the Triune God, as the Head over all things to the new Creation, He Himself makes known the character of its glory as being from God. "If any man is in Christ, He is a new creature (or, as in the margin of the R.V., "there is a new creation")... But all things are of God" (2 Cor. 5. 17, 18). Whatever place the Church occupies is due to Christ, and He both is the Source of it and gives it its true character.

(iii) The Second Aspect of His Resurrection: Revelation 1. 5.

This passage again speaks of Him as the Firstborn in connection with His death and resurrection. Here He is called "the Firstborn of the dead." There is no preposition in the original, according to the best MSS., in contrast to Colossians 1. 18, where the preposition *ek*, "out of," is used. Here, as there, the term does not bear the sense of primogeniture, but of priority, superiority, and Headship, in virtue of His relationship with the Father. The distinction between the two passages is this, that the phrase in Revelation 1. 5 lays special stress upon the fact that Christ *was* dead (cp. verse 18), while Colossians 1. 18 lays stress upon the fact that He rose from the *midst of* the dead. Just as in Colossians 1. 15, where the term "Firstborn" is used objectively to denote that Creation owes its existence to Him and is maintained under His dominating power, so here, the fact that the saints are to be raised from the dead is due to His resurrection. By reason of His resurrection His saints are called "the Church of the firstborn (ones) who are enrolled in Heaven" (Heb. 12. 23). For theirs is a position both of relationship to the Father and to the Son, and of pre-eminence in regard to others.

The firstborn in Israel were the representatives of the whole people as a nation set apart by God for Himself. Israel is similarly described as "My son, My firstborn" (Exodus 4. 22; cp. Jer. 31. 9). In each case the thought is that of pre-eminence in relationship to God. In regard to Israel, other nations are to be brought into Divine favour hereafter because of the relationship which God established between Himself and His chosen people. In this sense they are His firstborn.

We may compare the term "firstfruits," which signifies a special position as the outcome of the favour of God and His dealings of grace. Two Hebrew words are thus translated, one meaning the chief or principal part (Num. 18. 12; Prov. 3. 9, etc.); the other the earliest ripe part of the crop or of the tree (Exod. 23. 16; Neh. 10. 35, etc.); they are found together in Exodus 23. 19, etc.: "the first of the firstfruits."

As the whole land of Canaan was conse-
crated to God by the consecration of the
firstfruits, so the whole nation of Israel
was acknowledged as belonging to God
by the setting apart of the firstborn (Exod.
13. 12-16). Subsequently, the tribe of
Levi was substituted for the firstborn of
the families, to minister to the Lord
(Num. 3. 12, 45-50).

So the Church is the peculiar possession
of God. It is not His only possession,
but, as it is "the Church of the firstborn
ones, " they are, in their special relationship, a token that all else belongs to Him.
Their union with Christ in His resurrection
life obtains for them this distinction over
other members of the human race. The
title identifies them immediately with
Christ Himself. All others who are brought
into Divine favour are viewed in this term.
Just as Christ as "the Firstfruits" is the
earnest and pledge of the future resurrection of saints, so believers, "a kind of

firstfruits, " are the earnest and pledge of the eventual restoration of Creation.

(iv) His Position among the Glorified Saints: Romans 8. 29.

"Whom He foreknew, He also fore-ordained to be conformed to the image of His Son, that He might be the Firstborn among many brethren. " This points to the consummation of the Divine counsels in Christ, when, with bodies conformed to His body of glory, the saints will be in His complete likeness: "Whom He fore-ordained, them He also called: and whom He called, them He also justified: and whom He justified, them He also glorified" (v. 30). This past tense is prospective, the future event being presented as accomplished, in line with the preceding statements. That Christ is spoken of as "the Firstborn among many brethren" indicates that He is the pattern, or type, to which they are to be conformed in a relationship in which, since He is the only begotten Son, He stands in priority and superiority to them, and, being the Firstborn, He stands in His glorified position as pre-eminent over them. Their Divine relationship is a matter of pure grace. He will not stand alone, in His absolute, unoriginated glory as the only begotten Son ; on the contrary, Divine grace having related us to Him, He will be seen in His pre-eminence as the Firstborn among those whom "He is not ashamed to call His brethren," the many sons who will have been brought to glory through His death. In that consummation of grace He will say, "Behold, I and the children which God hath given Me" (Heb. 2. 10-13).

(v) His Manifested Glory:
Hebrews 1. 6.

In point of time the last passage in which Christ is called "the Firstborn" is

Hebrews 1. 6: "And when He again bringeth in the Firstborn into the world (the habitable earth), He saith, And let all the angels of God worship Him. "

The R.V. rendering is important for a proper understanding of the meaning. The word *palin*, "again, " is not used in verse 6 in the same way as in verse 5, to introduce an additional quotation. In verse 6 it comes, in the original, inside the adverbial clause which begins with the word "when. " Another instance of this use of the word is in 2 Corinthians 12. 21, "when I come again. "

Accordingly, in verse 6, instead of simply introducing a fresh quotation, it points to the future event, when God will again bring His Firstborn into the world, that is to say, at the Second Advent. The time referred to is marked by the Divine decree: "And let all the angels of God worship Him. " At His birth there was "a multitude of the Heavenly host praising God"

(Luke 2. 13), but upon His return to the earth in His manifested glory, all the angels will worship Him. They will accompany Him when He comes in the glory of His Father (Matt. 16. 27; 25. 31; 2 Thess. 1. 7; Rev. 19. 14). Now the quotation, "Let all the angels of God worship Him," is from the Septuagint Version of Deuteronomy 32. 35-43. That passage speaks of the time of the Second Advent. It tells of the judgment of the foes of Israel, the final deliverance of that nation, and the blessing granted to the Gentiles. The Septuagint is frequently quoted in the New Testament.

The following is a rendering of the salient parts of the passage: "In the day of vengeance I will recompense. For the Lord shall be comforted over His servants. For I will sharpen My sword like lightning . . . and I will render judgment to Mine enemies, and will recompense them that hate Me. . . . My sword shall devour flesh

. . . from the blood of the wounded . . . from the head of their enemies that rule over them. . . . Rejoice ye heavens with Him, and let all the angels of God worship Him; rejoice ye Gentiles with His people . . . the Lord shall purge His people's land." The head of the enemies of Israel, as in the R. V. of verse 42, "the head of the leaders of the enemy," is the man of sin, the first beast of Revelation 13. With this prophecy may be compared Psalms 96 to 100; Isaiah 11. 4; Daniel 7. 11; Zechariah 14; 2 Thessalonians 2. 8; Revelation 19. 20, and other passages relating to the circumstances of Christ's Second Advent.

The Five Passages Reviewed.

To summarise the five passages, He Who was the Father's Firstborn before the creation of the Universe, to which He Himself gave being, He Who is the "Firstborn from the dead," "the Firstborn among many brethren," will, when He

comes to overthrow the foes of God and
of His people the Jews, and to set up His
Kingdom of peace upon the earth, occupy,
as the Firstborn, His pre-eminent position
in the very place of His former humiliation
and rejection.

Distinguishing, then, between the two
titles, "Only begotten" and "Firstborn,"
the former speaks of His unoriginated
relationship to God the Father, as expressive of His delight in His Son, and
looks beyond the limits of human thought
to the eternity of the past. Referring
as it does to His Divine, unique, and
absolute relationship, it is not used with
reference to created beings. The title
"Firstborn" is used, however, with reference to created beings, but distinguishes
Him (1) from all creatures absolutely,
and (2) relatively from those who form
the Church and will be brought into the
glory of complete conformity to His likeness. The fourfold teaching of the title

may be set forth thus: it indicates (1) His Divine relationship, a relationship essential and unoriginated in itself; (2) His priority to created beings in the matter of time; (3) His creative power as the Source of their existence; (4) His pre-eminence and Headship over them, He being the ideal type Whose glory they are designed to set forth, in being conformed thereto.

"The Image of the Invisible God."

The mention of Christ as the Firstborn with regard to Creation in Colossians 1. 15 has a special significance in connection with the preceding statement, "Who is the image of the invisible God." That predicates His Deity. For *eikōn*, "image," is not mere likeness or resemblance, it involves visible and adequate representation. Thus, when used of Christ, it expresses in the one word what is said of Him in John 1. 18, with regard to the Father, that "He hath declared Him;"

that is to say, has visibly and completely represented Him. Its use in Hebrews 10. 1, in contrast to *skia*, "a shadow," suggests the idea of substance. The Law had "a shadow of the good things to come, not the very image of the things," *i.e.*, not the substance of the things themselves.

With this in view, then, He is called "the Firstborn of every creature" (the absence of the article before "Firstborn" throwing stress upon this relationship to the Father, see p. 19). Now the Epistle to the Colossians was written to counteract the heretical teachings promulgated in Western Asia and elsewhere, that matter was the origin and abode of evil, that therefore God and matter were antagonistic to each other, and had no communication with each other, and that the creation and government of the world were due to the agency of a series of intermediate beings, angels, or emanations, acting as mediators.

To combat these speculative errors, the
apostle sets forth the truth that Christ,
the Firstborn, the one Eternal Son, was,
as such, the sole mediatorial Agent both
in Creation and in the maintenance of the
Universe, and is, likewise, as the Firstborn (with the significance of the term as
mentioned), the one Mediator in regard to
the spiritual creation, the Church. Just
as later on, in instructing Timothy, who
was working in that very district, as to
what he was especially to inculcate, he
says, "For there is one God, one Mediator
also between God and Men, Himself Man,
Christ Jesus" (1 Tim. 2. 5). Just as,
again, the apostle John, combating the
same error, shows that the eternal Word,
the only begotten Son, became Incarnate,
for the purposes of redemption. The eternal Son was the one answer to all cosmical
speculations, the solution to all mystical
problems.

While creation was a mediatorial act,

and Christ is also the one Mediator in regard to redemption and the spiritual creation, the subject of His Mediatorship is not actually mentioned in the Gospel of John. This omission is appropriate to that special feature of this Gospel, which sets forth believers as children of God. Christ is the Mediator of the Covenants (Gal. 3. 19, 20; Heb. 8. 6; 9. 15; 12. 24); He is the Mediator between God and men; He will be the Mediator of the Kingdom of God in its future phase (1 Cor. 15. 24-28). But He is not said to be the Mediator between God the Father and His children.

Chapter VI

"IN HIM WAS LIFE"

CHAPTER VI

"In Him was Life"

LIKE the Father, the Son has life in Himself, as being one with Him in the Godhead. "In Him was life" (John 1. 4). He is "the Life" (11. 25; 14. 6; 1 John 5. 20). Yet the life essentially in Him was not possessed independently of the Father. He says, "As the Father hath life in Himself, even so gave He to the Son to have life in Himself" (5. 26). The very comparison, "As the Father hath life in Himself," precludes the idea that the Lord was referring simply to the human life upon which He entered at His birth. It is not a case of cause and effect, or of consequence upon a condition. In other words, the statement does not convey the idea that since the Father hath life in Himself, on that account **He** gave to the Son to have life in Himself. The statement is one of comparison; the measure of the life of the Son is the measure of the life of the Father. The Father did not give life to the Son as He gives it to creatures. The unity of the two Persons in the Godhead forbids the thought. Life essentially resides in the Son, and has ever done so, as One possessing an eternal communication of it from the Father, in virtue of the unoriginated relationship in the Godhead.

The special tense of the verb in the original rendered "gave" (the aorist, which is, literally, the undefined tense) is not here equivalent to the perfect tense, "He hath given."*

---

*The aorist tense in Greek is the normal method of expressing "indefinite or undefined action." It is often culminative, not expressing action from the point of view of an act carried out at a precise or definite occasion, but describing an event as a whole without reference to the time taken in its accomplishment. "The Greek aorist takes no note of any interval between itself (*i.e.*, what is **ex-**

That the Son has life from the Father
cannot be dissociated from the eternal
relationship.   It has been well said, "The
Father from all eternity giveth it, the Son
from all eternity receiveth it. "   That the
Lord Jesus is the Giver of life to man does
not rest simply and solely upon the fact
that He became Man with a view to giving
Himself in propitiatory sacrifice.   Eternal
life is bestowed indeed on that ground,
but that not without the primary and
essential fact that the Son was co-eternal
and co-existent with the Father in life
and relationship.   So with reference to

---

pressed in the tense) and the moment of speaking. . . . The
Greek aorist and the English past do not exactly correspond.
. . . The aorist is so rich in meaning that the English labours
to express it. " (A. T. Robertson's Grammar of the Greek
New Testament, pp. 831, 832, 848).

If this is so in natural circumstances and conditions, how
much more in matters concerning the inscrutable relationships in the Godhead and conditions relative to the life of the
Persons in the Godhead.   We have no hesitation therefore
in regarding the use of the aorist tenses in John 5. 26 and
27 as pointing, not to specific events in time, but to that
which lies beyond time limitations, and appertains to the
Divine and eternal counsels in view of the Incarnation of
the Son and His redemptive work and judicial functioning.

the same use of the word "gave" in the next verse, where the Lord says, "And He gave Him authority to execute judgment because He is the Son of Man." The giving of authority to Him to execute judgment is indeed in view of His being the Son of Man as well as the Son of God, but no specific point of time is indicated as to the giving. It does not say that the Father gave this authority to the Son after He had become Son of Man. We gather, then, that His statement is to be viewed in the eternal light of the counsels of God, with Whom the future is as real and assured as the present. *

The opening of the First Epistle of John gives further testimony to the Lord's pre-existent Sonship. The apostle says, "We . . . declare unto you the life, the eternal life, which was with the Father

---

*That He is the Son of God conveys the fact of His essential Deity; that He is the Son of Man expresses not simply His humanity, but the fact that He is ideally the representative Man, fulfilling in His Person the Divine purposes regarding man.

and was manifested unto us." That the eternal life is the Person of our Lord Jesus Christ is clear not only from the context, which shows that He was one Whom the apostles had seen and handled, but from the identification of "the Eternal Life" with Christ, in what is said at the end of the Epistle, namely, "We are in Him that is true, even in His Son Jesus Christ. This is the true God and eternal life." As "the eternal life," He was with "the Father." The apostle does not here say that He was with God, but with "the Father." Not that He was in the eternal past with One Who subsequently became the Father at the Incarnation, but that, as "the Life," He was with One Who stood to Him in the relationship of Father. The manifestation was temporal, the presence with the Father was eternal. He did not begin to be the Life at His birth, neither did He then begin to be the Son.

CHAPTER VII

———

SOME FURTHER PASSAGES WITH REFERENCE TO GOD AS "THE FATHER"

CHAPTER VII

Some Further Passages with Reference to God as "The Father"

The Father and Every Fatherhood.

IN Ephesians 3. 14, the apostle addresses God as "the Father from Whom (*ek*, expressing the Source) every family (*margin*, fatherhood) in Heaven and on earth is named. "

While there is considerable manuscript evidence for the addition, as in the A.V., of "our Lord Jesus Christ, " yet the weight of MS. evidence is for its omission. Even were it otherwise, and the text were read as in the A.V., the doctrine that the Divine relationship between the Father and the Son began at the Incarnation could not be maintained from this passage. The classes of beings mentioned as a "family," or "fatherhood" (*patria*) derive their name from their relation to the Father (*patēr*). While it sometimes signifies lineage from the Father's side, it stands also for the individuals who claim a common father, as in Luke 2. 4 (family), or again, for a number of families descended from a common stock (Acts 3. 25). In the language of the Septuagint, *e.g.*, 1 Chron. 16. 28 and Psalm 22. 28, the tribes of the Israelites were divided further into families.

Accordingly, what are spoken of here as fatherhoods in Heaven and on earth derive their character as such from God, as the Father, and since He is spoken of in this way with regard to classes of beings which so existed before the Incarnation, His title Father is here independent of the Incarnation. Now the title "the Father" is a relative term, and involves the existence of the Son. Hence this Divine relationship forms the basis upon which the fatherhood characterising the classes of the beings referred to exists, and this basis of relationship in the Godhead is not conditioned by circumstances of time, but is a matter of eternity. That every fatherhood "is named" from the Father expresses that the characteristics which make it what it is are derived from, and are therefore conformed to, Him. *

The Father as the Disposer of Times and Seasons.

When, at the last of His series of manifestations to the disciples, they asked the Lord whether He would at that time restore the Kingdom to Israel, He said,

---

*There are intimations in the Old Testament that the relationship of a family, or fatherhood, to God as the Father, existed before the Incarnation. Thus there was a time long before the birth of Christ when "All the sons of God shouted for joy" (Job 38. 7; cp. 1. 6; Psa. 89. 6, *margin*). God is spoken of as the Father of Israel in Deuteronomy 32. 6, and is addressed as such in Isaiah 63. 16 and 64. 8, while in Jeremiah 31. 9 He says again, "I am a Father to Israel, and Ephraim is My Firstborn."

"It is not for you to know times or seasons,
which the Father hath set within His own
authority" (Acts 1. 7).   Here again the
title, "the Father" is significant.   The
"times and seasons" comprehend all the
various epochs from the beginning of the
Divine arrangements in regard to the
world, throughout the periods of human
history therein.   The Lord does not say
that God, as such, has set them within
His own authority, but that "the Father"
hath done so.   Taken together with other
Scriptures, such as Colossians 1. 15, 16,
the intimation in this title of relationship
is not that it began with the Incarnation,
as if the Lord is speaking of the Disposer
of the times and seasons, as One Who
became His Father at His birth, but that
they have from the beginning received their
dispositions from Him as "the Father."

"To the Glory of God the Father."

The confession that Jesus Christ is Lord

is to be made by every tongue, "to the glory of God the Father" (Phil 2. 11). This latter title, forming the climax to the whole passage, from verses 6 to 11, is used absolutely of God in His relationship to Christ, and not relatively to His birth. The passage stresses His unoriginated equality with God, His voluntary condescension and obedience even unto death, and the Divine act in highly exalting Him. His condescending stoop is here mentioned as His own act, and this is deeply significant. We will consider the various clauses of this passage.

"Being in the form of God, " He "counted it not a prize to be on an equality with God. " The word "being" translates the verb *huparchō*, which signifies "to exist originally. " It also conveys the fact that what a person was before the fact mentioned he continued to be after it. The word "form" translates the word *morphē*, which denotes, not a resemblance

or shape, but all that is essential to anything. Thus this is true of Christ in
respect of His Deity, both in the eternal
past and in His Incarnation. While yet
in the glory with the Father He "counted
it not a prize," or rather, "a thing to be
grasped" (see margin) to be on an equality
with God.

Instead of counting it something to
be grasped to be on an equality with God,
He "emptied Himself, taking the form of
a servant, becoming (see margin) in the
likeness of men."

As we have noticed, these two latter
clauses are explanatory of the statement:
"He emptied Himself" (see p. 57). The
margin "becoming" gives the rendering
of *genomenos*. It does not signify that
He "was made," but expresses what was
His own self-emptying act. The word
rendered "likeness" (*homoiōma*) expresses
again not mere resemblance, but the reality
of His humanity.

Further, "being found in fashion as a man, He humbled Himself, becoming obedient even unto death, yea, the death of the Cross." The first clause expresses not simply His humanity, but the fact that He was at the same time the Incarnate Son of God.

The word *schēma*, "fashion," again signifies the reality of His humanity, but with this additional thought, that in the state and relations of men He was revealed and was recognised as such. The word *genomenos*, rightly rendered "becoming," is the same as in the preceding verse, and further expresses His voluntary act. In His subjection to the Father's will, He became obedient "even unto death." The word "even" is useful, as it obviates any idea that death was His master. This becoming obedient is expressive of the way in which He humbled Himself.

"Wherefore also God highly exalted Him, and gave unto Him the Name which

is above every name; that in the Name of
Jesus every knee should bow, of things in
Heaven and things on earth and things
under the earth, and that every tongue
should confess that Jesus Christ is Lord,
to the glory of God the Father. " This title
"God the Father" covers the whole passage.
The single title God is used before in the
passage, not only in verse 6, in describing
that Christ was in the form of God, and
counted it not a thing to be grasped to be
on an equality with God, but also in verse
9, which describes the act of God in highly
exalting Him.   It was "God the Father"
as such Who highly exalted Him, and it
was "God the Father" with Whom He
was on an equality before He emptied
Himself.   The worship given to Christ is
likewise given to the Father, for the Son
is one in nature with Him.

Index of Subjects